Big Machines At Work

Earthmovers

By Hal Rogers

SCHOLASTIC INC.

New York   Toronto   London   Auckland   Sydney
Mexico City   New Delhi   Hong Kong   Buenos Aires

For information regarding permission, write to:
The Child's World®, Inc.
P.O. Box 326
Chanhassen, Minnesota 55317

Photos: © 1998 David M. Budd Photography

ISBN 0-439-65047-X

Printed in the U.S.A.
First Scholastic printing, February 2004

Contents

On the Job

On the job, earthmovers work at a **construction site.** They move dirt from one place to another.

An earthmover has giant tires.

It can travel across rough ground.

A **blade** scoops up dirt as the machine

moves. The blade is like a shovel.

The dirt goes into a big bin. It is called a **can.** The can is full now. Some dirt spills over the side.

The earthmover scoops up dirt. It helps make the land flat. Workers cannot put up a building until the land is perfectly flat.

The earthmover dumps the dirt in a huge pile. Later, another machine will take the dirt away.

Sometimes an earthmover helps workers make a road. An earthmover can flatten a hill. It can also fill up a big hole.

Climb Aboard!

Would you like to see where the driver sits? An earthmover's driver is called an **operator.** The operator sits inside the **cab** and uses special **levers** to make the machine work. The driver steers the earthmover with a steering wheel.

Up Close

The inside

1. The operator's seat

2. The steering wheel

3. The levers

The outside

1. The cab

2. The can

3. The blade

23

Glossary

blade (BLAYD)
The blade is a long metal scoop on an earthmover. It picks up dirt like a shovel.

cab (KAB)
A cab is the place where the driver sits. It has a seat, a steering wheel, and levers.

can (KAN)
The can is a big bin on an earthmover. It holds dirt after the blade scoops it up.

construction site (kun-STRUCK-shun SITE)
A construction site is a place where workers build something. Workers make buildings at a construction site.

levers (LEV-erz)
The earthmover's levers are metal bars with black knobs at the ends. The operator uses them to move the machine.

operator (OPP-er-ay-ter)
The operator is the person who drives the earthmover. He or she works the levers that make the machine move.